Welcome to Snack Time!

Dear Parents, Caregivers, and Teachers:

Blue's Clues is Nick Jr.'s think-along, play-along program for preschoolers. Our mission is to empower, challenge, and build the self-esteem of preschoolers while making them laugh. The activity book which you are about to open follows that same philosophy.

Blue's Clues utilizes a multi-layered approach to learning and playing. Every game, theme, and concept integrates levels of presentation which appeal to the full range of the target audience, 2–6 year olds.

Play these games with your children and remember, at **Blue's Clues**, we play to learn.

The **Blue's Clues**
Creative Team

Layout by Marcy Pritchard for Dog-Eared Design

Cover Design by Jenine Pontillo

Blue's Clues was created by Traci Paige Johnson, Todd Kessler, and Angela C. Santomero.

A special thanks to ACS, MS, and AW for all their creative talent.

Everyone coming to the party is bringing their favorite snacks to share.

Find all 3 clues hidden in this book to figure out what snack Blue is bringing to the party.

What number is Tickety's little hand pointing to ?

Can you help Blue set up for her snack party?

It looks like Blue is missing a balloon from one of her bunches.

Can you draw the missing balloon?

Can you finish setting the table?

What did Blue forget?

How many more apples does Shovel need to have the same number as Pail?

Can you draw them?

Do you know where oranges grow?

Do you know where grapes grow?

Where does orange juice come from?

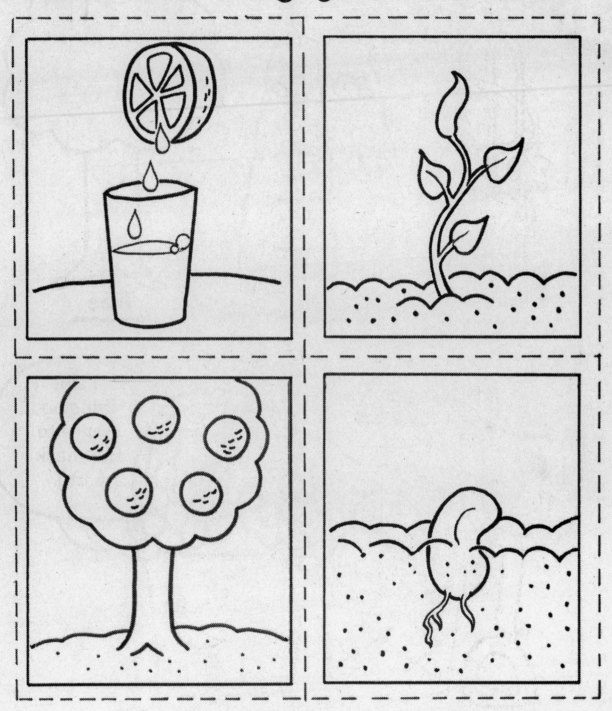

✂ Cut out the cards.

Can you put the cards in the right order?

Which snack doesn't belong?

Circle the item that is made from grapes.

Did you find your first clue?

Draw it on the notebook page.

Do you know what Blue is bringing to the snack party?

Circle the item that doesn't belong.

Can you color 10 candy canes for Gingerbread Boy?

Can you help Gingerbread Boy find his way to Blue's house?

Which drink does Baby Bear want to bring?

Which snack does Baby Bear want to bring?

Circle the picture that rhymes with the underlined word.

To Blue,

Snack party! Snack party! They're so much <u>fun</u>.

I hope it's not raining so we can
picnic in the _____.

Rain	Tree	Sun

Mr. Salt and Mrs. Pepper, they love to <u>bake</u>.
I hope they bring their special
banana _____.

Sock	Cake	Pumpkin

Paprika likes to eat foods that start with the letter <u>P</u>.

I wonder if Blue will bring a snack that starts
with the letter _____.

Q	F	B

Graham Crackers and milk is what
I'm going to <u>share</u>.
From your good pal _____.

Baby Bear	Slippery	Tickety

Do you know what time Tickety's ice pops will be ready?

Did you find your second clue?

Draw it on the notebook page.

Do you know what Blue is bringing to the snack party?

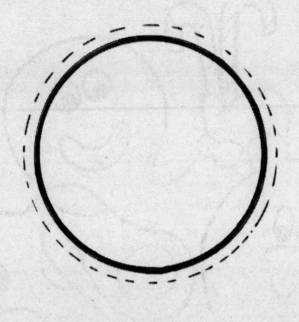

 Color these shapes and cut them out.

Save them to help the Felt Friends later.

✂ **Color these shapes and cut them out.**

Save them to help the Felt Friends later.

It's the Felt Friends!

What shapes make up Freddy's lollipop?

Use your shapes to make a lollipop for Fifi.
Paste them on this page.

What shapes make up Fifi's ice cream cone?

Use your shapes to make an ice cream cone for Freddy.
Paste your shapes on this page.

 Cut out the recipe cards.

Can you put the cards in the right order so we can make cupcakes?

Draw what's missing.

Banana

Eggs

Sock

BAKING SODA

SUGAR

FLOUR

Orange

BUTTER

Horn

Can you circle the items that we need to make banana cake?

Can you follow the patterns to help Mr. Salt and Mrs. Pepper finish decorating the banana cake?

Paprika likes snacks that start with the letter P!

Apple

Pineapple

Watermelon

Pretzel

Pear

Pie

Cookie

Use your purple crayon to circle all the snacks that start with the letter P.

What do you want to bring to Blue's snack party?

Draw your favorite snack!

Did you find your last clue?

Draw it on the notebook page.

Do you know what Blue is bringing to the snack party?

Can you count Slippery's bubbles?

Can you use all 3 clues to figure out what Blue is bringing to the snack party?

Cheese

Circle

Tomato

Draw your answer to
Blue's Clues!

Pizza!

Can you help Blue finish topping her pizza?

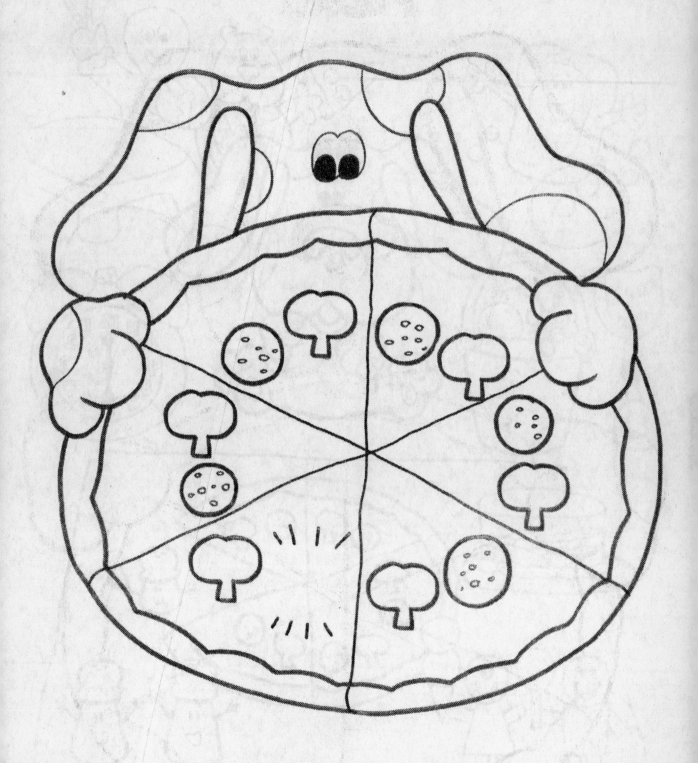

Follow the pattern!

What did each friend bring to the snack party?

Draw a picture of yourself.

Your favorite snack.

 Cut out the cards and match them.

figured out

BLUE'S CLUES

I am really smart!